LOUISE
IN LOVE

Also by Mary Jo Bang

Apology for Want

LOUISE
IN LOVE

{POEMS}

by

MARY JO BANG

GROVE PRESS

New York

Published simultaneously in Canada
Printed in the United States of America

FIRST EDITION

Library of Congress Cataloging-in-Publication Data

Bang, Mary Jo.
    Louise in love : poems / by Mary Jo Bang.
        p. cm.
    ISBN 0-8021-3760-1
    I. Title.
    PS3552.A47546 L68 2001
    811'.54—dc21   00-057794

Design by Julie Duquet

Grove Press
841 Broadway
New York, NY 10003

01 02 03 04   10 9 8 7 6 5 4 3 2 1

for TIMOTHY BERNARD DONNELLY

CONTENTS

ACKNOWLEDGMENTS

Grateful acknowledgment is made to the editors of the following journals in which these poems, sometimes in an earlier version, first appeared:

Conduit: "Louise," "Oh, Dear, What Can the Matter Be," "Too Late, Louise Said, Means," and "What Is a Mouth?";

Denver Quarterly: "Ritual Gestures" and "They Were That and Then";

Fence: "The Dog Bark";

Gettysburg Review: "The Ana of Bliss";

Harvard Review: "That Was All, Louise Said, Except For";

Jacket: "The Diary of a Lost Girl," "The Penguin Chiaroscuro," "The Medicinal Cotton Clouds Come Down to Cover Them," "Dark Smudged the Path Untrammeled," and "A Hurricranium, He Said";

Kenyon Review: "Travel Is Easy by Train," "Kiss, Kiss, Said Louise, by Way of a Pay Phone," and "Does Mrs. Hunt Tear Linen Straight as Ever?";

New American Writing: "A Cake of Nineteen Slices" and "Louise Sighs, Such a Long Winter, This";

The New Republic: "Like a Fire in a Fire" and "Time Speeds, Said Louise, When a Fever Rises";

The New Yorker: "The Star's Whole Secret";

Paris Review: "She Couldn't Sing At All, At All," "So This," and "The Still Knife Still Suspended";

Partisan Review: "Night Falling Fast";

Ploughshares: "Ham Paints a Picture to Illustrate an Early Lesson: O Trauma!";

Poetry Review: "To Savor the Sequel" and "Etched, Tetched, Touched";

Slope: "In the Quieter Aftermath";

TriQuarterly: "Here's a Fine Word: Prettiplease" and "The Raven Feeds Reynard";

Verse: "Belle Vue" and "Enchained";

Yale Review: "Night and Nail."

"The Dog Bark," "Like a Fire in a Fire," "Louise in Love," and "The Star's Whole Secret" appeared in *The Bread Loaf Anthology of New American Poets*, Michael Collier, ed. (University Press of New England, 2000).

Many of these poems were written during a period of residency at Princeton University made possible by a Hodder Fellowship awarded by the Council for the Humanities, for which I am extremely grateful. Thanks are also owed to The Corporation of Yaddo and to the Chateau Lavigny for residencies. For suggestions and encouragement along the way, many thanks to Stephen Burt, Claudia Rankine, Monica de la Torre, Mac Wellman, and Mark Wunderlich. And special (and eternal) thanks to Richard Howard for his confidence in my work. "Ham Paints a Picture to Illustrate an Early Lesson: O Trauma!" is for Michael Van Hook.

The italicized lines in "Does Mrs. Hunt Tear Linen Straight as Ever?" come from letters of John Keats [to his brothers (15 April 1817); to Leigh Hunt (10 May 1817)]. The italicized lines in "That Was All, Louise Said, Except For" come from *Mrs. Dalloway* by Virginia Woolf. The italicized lines in "And No Sign Will Mark the Midpoint's Passing" are adapted from an incantation to the Babylonian goddess, Ishtar. "Night and Nail" contains deliberate, but slanted, echoes of Keats's "Ode to a Nightingale." "Enchained" borrows the phrase "Much have I travell'd" from Keats's "On First Looking Into Chapman's Homer." The italicized lines in "Raptured" come from Book II of Keats's "Hyperion: A Fragment." The italicized lines in "Interrupted Briefly by a Borrowed Phrase, the Scene Proceeds" come from Book I of Keats's "Hyperion: A Fragment."

DRAMATIS PERSONAE

LOUISE

LYDIA, *sister of Louise*

HAMILTON GORDON III (HAM)

CHARLES GORDON, *brother of Ham*

ISABELLA, *a child*

THE OTHER

ECLIPSED

The crimped beige of a book, turned-down corner.
The way an eclipse begins with the moon
denting the sun's liquid disk, taking a first bit
then more and more and. Leaving a regal rim, a dim
spared portion, a shiver. How cold she was
as the cloud covered the cuckoo-land,
birds batting the tree fringe. Fitful caprice.
Foolish, yes, they were, those birds, but clever too.
A nostrum of patterning rain had fallen
beforehand ceding the hibiscus buds bundled
and in disarray. In the news p. Nostradamic foretelling
of retinal damage written in novelese.
Wasn't the skeptic invented to nourish an interest in science?
Yes. The puma swallows the sun, only to spit it back out.
Diaphragmatic heaving. Base emetic act.
The puky little sun glowing to a glare. Puissance.
One's own right hand teaching one to look, to see, to leap
upon some notional premise.
Louise placed the next-to-night glasses on the table.
It is, she said, so over. But it wasn't.
Specters they would be
rooted eighty-two years in the same spot waiting
for another and then an offhand remark and one by one
(which is the way death takes us, he said)
they took their shadows
and went out of the garden and into the house.

SHE COULDN'T SING AT ALL, AT ALL

Louise said. No subtle cadences capturing birdnote
nor the melancholic "My Love
Is in a Light Attire." She could speak well enough
but to sing was to vivisect the ear's dear pleasure desired.
Ham suggested canasta
or a hike to a hillock. The other reminded
no night-over camping—Lydia was soundly allergic to that.
Charles Gordon proposed
a boat ride to a big, big lake and a stroll
in the Parc d'Avenir. They heard an April angelus tolling its sixes,
a sure sign that the winter demon was down.
It was now a matter of waiting
for the haughty naughty beguilement of warmth.
They were standing on the balcony when
Louise was tossed not a rose or two with flayed edges
but an entire bouquet of hibiscus (a horde of bishops
huddling at the heart of each). Below them, a boy sweeping—
sheep, sheep, sheep—looked up
and souffled Lydia a kiss. Oh, it would be a good day, wontn't it?
Life flung riverward and on and on
the baby boat floating, spinning in the hope current,
someone singing "Sometimes a bun, sometimes only a
      biscuit."

THE DOG BARK

Louise peered into the corner of the cabinet
of fossilized delights: mandragon manikin, a dried mermaid,

assorted dog barks of crass appetites.
It was six and dark early. Don't forget numbers, Ham said,

are only examples: one and two with their sterile marriage,
three with its tattooed face. That year the gifts were lustrous:

a bear with the head of a horse, small nipples, flowers
in its ears. Louise said, Who doesn't love

the sound of scissor snips and free-for-all terms of endearment?
The dog, they named *Lucky*

To Be Alive, and refused to let it be altered.

BELLE VUE

Gorgeous that pillar, that post—both spiraled
with lashes of laurel. And between the two, four
couples fashioned past fumble.

The party wanted the night
sand to swallow their prints so they drove to the beach.
Back home, the filament blinked in the lamp

by which Louise sat reading a book about sleep.
Six knobs controlled the night but the day,
the day, she read, was rudderless,

an eggbreak knowing no bounds but becoming
an edgeless eye fluttering open at the sound of a siren,
a peony shaken—each petal a shower of instant truths.

Wake up. One wanted to hear
the sky—a river turned sidewise.
The wrist's tiny veinlets sunk

while gravity's gooseherd gathered the minion
capillaries. Wake up, wake up. The filament flickered again,
a forecast for certain. Sunrise would be

. . .

riddled with sound. At irregular intervals, rain.
The same letters one day would read
Charlotte; Charcot, the next; and then

charcuterie. Coincidence.
A grid over every window erased by the lack
of light.

In the everworld of art, even the lettuces' red leaves
stayed suspended between dissolves. Eye and idea, a rope
at the waist. She was held—

not by the text, but by the pretty pictures.

THE STAR'S WHOLE SECRET

Did she drink tea? Yes, please. And after,
the halo of a glass gone.
A taxi appeared out of elsewhere.

Five constellations, Louise said,
but only two bright stars among them. Soon, Ham said,
the whale will reach the knot of the fisherman's net;

the moon will have its face in the water.
And we'll all feel the fury of having been used
up in maelstrom and splendor.

Mother did say, Louise said, try to be popular,
pretty, and charming. Try to make others
feel clever. Without fear, what are we?

the other asked. The will, said Louise. The mill moth
and the lavish wick, breathless in the remnant
of a fire.

KISS, KISS, SAID LOUISE,
BY WAY OF A PAY PHONE

To the other who'd been left behind.
The city was unlucky in cloudy and chance of.
Routing the enemy, following a route.

What does it mean, Mary Louise,
that the mall in Midcreek will open in May?
They were getting away

to nature, conveyance as a form of diffidence.
Every avenue, said Ham, still ends at perception.
There is a point, said Louise, when one will act or won't

even know what she's missed.
She was wearing a wig and suit of blue serge
and looked somewhat like that section

of a symphony written in the alphabet soup
of C and B-neath. The road was a ribbon
on the bright canyon bed. Clever twin, said Louise,

to those who know how to follow
a scheme that avoids the end of the senses
before there can be a begun. She saw: a blue car leaving

. . .

at three; a blue car returning at four; an odd-looking man
leaning against an ornamental Japanese pine.
They stopped at the house on the top of the hill,

lit like a candle-house cake. I hope, Ham said,
there's a fire station deep in this forest.
Forest? What forest? she said.

Don't you see—
it's a fantastic sea where nothing but nothing can save us.

THE DIARY OF A LOST GIRL

Four diphtheria deaths, then fire, now five named lakes
with tranquil looks. Yet rampantly mad.
A lunatic shriek from a ruffian

child. One oar wrestled a mob of shore fringe, another,
the wet underbirth. And madness,
was it afflicted by demons? Or stricken of God? Or vision,

thrown on an empty mirror, and there you were?
Later, upstairs—the lakes packed away
in pearly cases, the coppery spin of a high skyward

arrayed against a leaded window—the chiasmic
question recurred. She recalled shy little lessons
from a girl named Renee on the unattainable freedoms

of the flesh. In the dining room, they would crumple
over the table like paper angels
if anyone raised an eyebrow.

Otherwise, they leaned against scenery—looking down
at their Bonniedale shoes
as if they were in love with nothing else.

THE ANA OF BLISS

Heat rush of heaving. The heart
throbbing in the inner ear, wrists twined
with a red thread of electricity, lustered response.

O Ham, she said, and swooned
in the rattled reunion and sudden summer
of thunder.

His mouth was the yes that was wished on,
feet angled in. He said, My but aren't we?
Si, she said, aren't I

a rampant array
of negatives bashed and belittled?
Come in, come in, my little passion flower, he would
    often say.

An elevator's assuasive ascent, Icarus clicks
between floors. A head turned
as she entered the door.

. . .

Did you hear what I said? he said. You would be
so easy to love. Indefatigable mortar—
bitumen or pitch. An irreversible welding.

Wasn't this
what is bliss?

A CAKE OF NINETEEN SLICES

She was aware of the alarm
clock in the throat of a buff-colored bird with black head.
It's lovely, isn't it, the way stasis and darkness
disappear at the rapids? Or change. Yes, change.
Do you want a slice of cake? I do, I do.
The boys broke into the mansion,
setting off bells that had just been installed.
I would like to show you that tree in the forest
where moss bleeds the bark in a most peninsular way.
Twelve years had been shed by the time it was over.
She stood on a rise overlooking a road
alongside a lake that flowed into another,
and another, and another like hours
babbling their latebreaky news.
And everything, Louise said, has its own specificity,
the bird is simply a bird, and thus.
Ditto the murmuring missionaries, their misguided zeal
that forever results in a hereness unused to its thisness,
a *real* of no real appeal.

LOUISE

It was sepia, Louise said with a hint of nostalgia. Henna, he'd said, after seeing a facsimile of the world-famous photo of the woman who had dyed her hair red. Down, she said, descending the rungs of the ladder that led them right to the door of new depths. Depiction, she said, surfacing in order to say it and fracturing the spell under which they swam in the moment that ended an eon ago. Swans, she said, referring to the needle-neck birds black and white that lined the aisle down which one walked to get to the river on which they were skating away.

LIKE A FIRE IN A FIRE

They were difficult to find. It was summer so
they were dust dry and sky blue. Lighter, liminal, quite likely
to follow a line completely lacking in depth.

Louise dreamed a clowder of cats was eating yesterday's dinner
of snapper and fennel. Ham dreamed a hand
was playing a tin-can piano note twice too many times.

The other lay awake listening to a radio static
at the base of the stapes deep in the damaged right ear.
Soon, August would trade its heat

for September's cool shroud. The loose weave, a seize, Louise said,
through which the tail will fall through: dysthymic October,
deathy November.

December, a drear pentimento—unveiling the mouth
at abeyance, the mind at undone. Boneheap, rock beach,
birdie girls crooning in swan-feathered caps.

O seasons, O castles, Ham said, there's still the slight flutter
of blood in an outlying vein, light trained on a landscape
of shoulder with faint smell of soap.

DOES MRS. HUNT TEAR LINEN
STRAIGHT AS EVER?

Louise, lying half dressed on a hideabed, said
she wasn't going but the other insisted, so they all went
and inquired for the boat to the Isle.

They expected a dog with a magnificent hairdo
and a boy balleting over a roof, a circular saw
(buzzing, its affect).

Instead, they found *blooming Furze . . . a low Water
Water . . . one Nymph of Fountain,* swans ruminating,
ditto donkeys, men and women going gingerly along.

The wind threw a hissy fit and Louise grew vexed
and tired. These are not little instances, she said,
but possible outcomes of a story that cannot include us

(each to be ticked off in turn with an x'ed "Yes, go ahead"
or an absent "No, not yet").
Since the tale would advance without them,

she suggested they *procure some fatal scissors
and cut the thread* that held them there.
Does Mrs. S. cut bread and butter neatly as ever?

the other asked. And Ham cried out, *à propos of nothing,
For God's Sake, let us sit upon the Ground!*

17

TIME SPEEDS, SAID LOUISE,
WHEN A FEVER RISES

A phantasmagorical twilight outlined the skyscape:
a braced structure of cases and frames.
You look tired, the other noted.

And the saying, of course, made it so.
She was now in high dudgeon. What she needed, she said,
was caprice and a cocktail shaker.

A slim satin dress sewn tighter than truth.
The danger of languid and largo, Ham said,
was that of an egg left leaning against a white wall.

He suggested the game where giraffe meant mischief
caused by absence of thought; octopus: deep end,
a downfall. Fan: flirtation; comb: a false friend.

A fork in the shadow of a cup denoted conclusion
was about to be reached. Of course, the practice was more
than the theory and some symbols doubled the odds:

acorn, for example, could be either instant success
or someone would soon burn a bridge.

LOUISE IN LOVE

Much had transpired in the phantom realm:
Are we whole now? Louise asked.
I think we are, the other said.

And from the mirror: no longer blue in the face, and vague;
only destiny's dove bending a broke wing and beckoning.
The ride had been open and long, the car resplendent.

What rapture, this rode into sunset. This elegant end
where a band tugs a sleeve,
a hand labors with an illusion

of waving away a thread. And then they came to something
big: down the block, winking red lights and a crowd
of compelling circumference.

They were one with the woman, her rosacea face,
the snapdragon terrier, ten men in black helmets, a man supine
on a stretcher. O the good and the evil of accident.
. . .

They were wary, and justifiably so. The mind says no,
Louise admitted, but the heart, it loves repetition
and sport:

cat's paw from under the bedskirt,
dainty wile, frayed thing,
fish hook.

OH, DEAR, WHAT CAN THE MATTER BE

Louise let the other go first.
They passed through the turnstile singly: one sheep,
two sheep. It was too too much:
the meek hand on a banister,

eventual pigeons insisting first this way, then that.
Music coursed a curtained sidewalk.
She'd like to escape into it, but today was a turncoat.
Was this *fair*? Gravity holding her

while silence egged her on.
Amazing, she said, how even the bound foot walks
in a pinch, an economical shuffle—
draggle and scrape. And the mind never rests;

even in sleep, it mimes mother or mayhem.
A moment of abstraction
and the green stain on a wall becomes a relief map
of Kansas. Listen!

Were those the strings of an orchestra?
Or the melody of a coming attraction?
Louise sighed. It is true, she said,
some sums are not easy to reckon.

THAT WAS ALL, LOUISE SAID, EXCEPT FOR

The dalliance of spring-
boards, the lingering impression of an off-black blouse.
Facts, said Ham, too often confide an edifice
with no hint of what hides behind.

They had just come from seeing the clairvoyant.
She told them that like Clint Eastwood,
Louise had been born on an eclipse.
Since her moon was in Sagittarius, she could live

in a foreign country if ever she chose. In the cafe,
the service was slow: the waitress had taken up smoking
and a bald man was asking for more.
Across the street, a building stood facing its final demise.

A mud-spattered window in a double-hung door
was all that divided outside from in.
To Louise, the conversation seemed all too familiar—
I feel, she said to the other, like a sheet grown soft

with the deadweight of difficult sleep. She turned her head
(*She was like a poplar, she was like a river, she was*
like a hyacinth . . .).
What you are, said Ham, is beauty.

Empty, she said. No inbreath, no eyeblink.

AND NO SIGN WILL MARK THE
MIDPOINT'S PASSING

You will go on a long journey. Louise first heard it said
behind a curtain of bead. Then came a need to know how
and now to wander an empty room, asking:

Is this to be believed? Green water leaning
against an immovable tree. A tack in her shoe
had shimmied its way to the top.

The eyes, she said, on a well-behaved route
are ultimately blind. The lung, quite naturally,
is a rooted structure.

Who sleeps, goddess of love and war.
Harlot and pure, storehouse and empty.
Her breast a stone bowl, her shoulders clean, and uncovered.

She lay on her back, receiving the silk drip of sleep
as it was poured from above. Over her, stars
being made—hydrogen cooling in columns of ash,

. . .

diamonds condensing. Awake, she said,
I love shaping my mouth, then waiting to speak.
The day was subsiding like the small drama of a drawer

pushed into an oncoming slot.
On a shelf, oddments took up an overlay of dust. The bed
by the window caught whatever bit of weather came its way.

SHE LOVED FALLING

A car was coming to pick her up.
In order not to waste moments, Louise was making a fuss
with a feather duster, plumage relieved from a pheasant.

She was making a most unpleasant mess,
banishing dust motes from light-laden beams.
She stopped to slip

the canary bird back in its cage,
remodeling its feathers with the back of her fingers.
Nothing in nature alarmed her.

A bow in the shape of a butterfly festooned her blunt cut.
Last night she had fainted, revived in time
to see a fixed star flickering behind the frill

of four green fronds banded together
by a cheap rubber band. The faint had been a falling,
sudden and tender as the doctor in leather

. . .

who crossed the room to come to her aid. He said he knew
all about critical care and the way lungs let air in and out.
Today, the temperature had declined

in the wake of a heat wave. Dawn had been admirably mired
in a message meant only for her. Here, it said, fall here.
Into love's sweet looking glass.

TO SAVOR THE SEQUEL

Both happy and simple sad, the hesitant gamut
of where the lovetrain could run—there and back, there
and back, followed by the predictable

fade-out and that might be savored as well, but not likely.
She compared it to dropping
through an infinitude of slow lacerations.

Love, love, love, love, love, love, love—
a hive hum ongoing in the hear ear.
How could that be a thing of pure pleasure?

A fast-footed dance down the hall
that gave onto a vast view of hell. A bell at the door,
a beloved's name just above it.

Come in, come in. And she did as always enter
and she wished as always after
that the sequel might be seen (might be felt) as a form

of recreation, a game tied by two match-match opponents
instead of a chair and a window,
a wisp of ice running through her. The on-going on-going,
. . .

she opened the window wider, picked up her pen.
Dear X. Dearest X. What was there to say?
She rose and would no longer write.

The impulse had leaped over an edge,
an undulate verge, ever near, into which would sometimes fall
a tear or two, and however many feelings.

TOO LATE, LOUISE SAID, MEANS

A given was given and then
it ventured across in response to an imploding code.
Something had happened; some things had happened.

Can replication ever *be* pure? Ham asked.
If only there were a god.
What do they have to cry over? she asked,

pointing at the weeping cabbage and the carrot dropped
from the hand of a rabbit. The painting didn't answer
back. She could cry, she said,

but what good would that do? Two years, she told herself,
it's another thing altogether. In the next painting,
a silver dot floated at the foot of a hill.

I take that to mean, she said,
that more of the hour is coming
to us. She said, A day divides itself, really:

. . .

three pieces of time with their petty, or is it pretty,
demarcations. Parcels sent
back or held over.

The next painting was entitled Nothing
Is New. Not the fingers of night nor the tightening of time.
Certainly not the inevitable acts of contrition.

HERE'S A FINE WORD: PRETTIPLEASE

Mrs. Donna spoke, saying it was all very clear.
In the long month of *Maggio,* Louise would be jailed
in a match that one might say was morbid—
as in attachment to one who would give not a fig
for the right to be near.

She wrote down a date
with an eight at the end. This, she said, means the end
will occur at a seaside resort, a respectable spa
where one eats in one's robe and takes side-by-side baths
in beds made of ready-mixed mud.

She said Louise should then proceed, designless
and dissident, to a place where unlikely glitter would drift
like snow in the May of a previous year. That's memory,
my dear, she said softly.
Listen, Louise told her, he gave me a pill,

saying, With this you'll taste of divinity. With this,
you'll be easy to love. He said, Lie down, and I did.

YOU COULD SAY SHE WAS WILLFUL, BUT COMPARED TO WHAT?

She was eating a yellow pear wrapped in tissue tinted wan green.
Surgery, she said, had cured her of an addiction
to objects. She described the dull knife

as both exact and imprudent. Now she suffered
slightly from a lulling amnesia. Her recall was jagged,
like topiary cleaved along a zigzag divide.

She was, however, quite sure she'd seen silver fish
caught in the twine of treetops.
Don't we all come from water? Ham asked.

A mad purple flood
heaving behind some sweet mother breast.
Now she worried the sun had baked her unfit to be kissed.

Bliss, she said, is best viewed through an absence
of terror. Wasn't drowning similar to sex?
A saltwater embrace
. . .

on a bed of seaweed, green ribbons circling her wrists.
Tapered raindrops in a windless falling.
That flooded city, she said, was foreign to my dearest

fantasy. At the end of the day, there was only a tin voice
giving the overview
of swing lights in the closet of night.

THE PENGUIN CHIAROSCURO

The acrobat on the rosinback circled the track
thrice, then threw her a kiss.
She could see how well he'd been taught.

He still practiced, he said,
in order to better deserve his burnished fate.
You are rehearsing for what

play part? she asked. The doll's house
gleamed in the small room until the lights were turned off.
Then sweet sweet sleep and the street–

lamp gave up a glimpse of a carnival larger than life.
The carousel's rotal motion took on speed, then halted.
The lights were turned off. Someone was herding

the bumper cars into the stream,
eyes bright in their fendered faces.
The day was dry. The eyes were locked

in their neat little coffins. The mind was struck
by needlespray. A cool soon (someone was speaking).
A change of clothes? the dream master asked.

. . .

Yes. She would be a blue new, the terrain of now,
a nice never waiting, one destined
for pleasure in that place between a small pinch of dusk

and the hey diddle diddle of dawn.
The kiss arrived just in time.
A breeze blew a window open on a distant afternoon.

THE MEDICINAL COTTON CLOUDS COME DOWN TO COVER THEM

To smother their smallness
in felt. Unsatisfied folds, filmic
emotion—remote, pale, and impalpable.
Each with their own secret
inflection of want.
There was no debate on this but merely a mood
shift when certain words were mentioned.
Inane nexus of speech, never quite capturing
the what invoked.
She slid her panties down over her hips.
The broidered hue of illusion,
idea drunk in the delicate gloom.
The picture of a hand becoming
a hand. Whose? Yes. Desire reworked stepwise,
a would weep. A was told and lying very still.
Was allowing just so to happen
to her. Neck nape a curve becoming
infinite abyss extended to wish, wish, wish,
and righty-o, a stunning result. Isn't that nice?
Rosey-o, rosey-o. She woke, took one look:
Oh, it's you. Yes. I thought I dreamed you.
Siren girls sang somewhere. Nice, she said. Nice.

THE STORY OF SMALL CARS

Consider, she said, the statue
in the cloister seen on Tuesday: fluted pilasters
and conch shells. Oh, pretty, pretty. A shaved forehead,
tight belt, missing limb.
Oh, crippled. Yes, very crippled. But not very real.

Louise took the train
of her black velvet dress and leaned across the table.
She was telling the story of small cars.
The tale concerned a dog with a tiny blue fez,
a girl named Clara who caught the trail of a smoky cigar

and followed it into catastrophe, a zoo
of undue proportion,
a small green car that ran up a line on a cheek
that had lain on a bedsheet too long.
It ended with the window that opened in, opening out

onto the end of looking. There, she said, the sky is
whatever one wishes. As she spoke,
the intangible drifted out beyond the vast
until it could no longer be seen but was still vaguely
        perceived—
and nowhere in the sensuous world a cause.

LEXICON LOUISE

Lexicon of appearance, the small mouth, a bow
on the present. Her face came unhinged
in a diptych mirror. Slow eyes,

their slotted indecision, wave of cool blue
wafting through four walled rooms.
At least two sides to each always, at least.

The dead must stay dead, she said,
past flesh bifurcating at bone rim,
past rattle and false growth of hair, the occasion

of eye cloud and blood congesting in hollows.
(Tell little Isabellita not to weep, Ham said,
the flowers were meant to fade. And the dried fronds

will unfold only *under* the water.)
The clock faced the night like a white coat
in a half-lit room. She had once watched

. . .

a thorax opened at autopsy, noted the liver as marble,
the lungs as a gray flannel suit. Felt the caustic
effects of the chemical on her eye's fishy underlids.

Vulnerable membrane of underside. Of nose, of throat.
Sways what, she wondered, on these actions?
The posthumous frown set in the center of the diamond.

LOUISE SIGHS, SUCH A LONG WINTER, THIS

Stone basin, stone breath, stone bric-a-brac,
but finally a gown
of ambiguity, shimmering and more fitting
than a shift of drear reason,

a Come in, come in. We're having a party.
There's dancing; there's petting
in the bedroom to the right. Inevitable light
in the morning. Who will refuse enthrallment?

To be free, Louise says, is to be undecided.
Come and kiss the linen scarf where it drapes
the dresser's grain.
See how well it holds what it's been given?

See the empty stems of what were roses
in the once-ago garden?
The mansion and mausoleum lake
where the boat turned under?

Dollish and dressed in pretense, Louise turns
to the window: in one eye, she sees fir trees
circling a suspicious white house,
a peevish pink shed; in the other, a helicopter

distinguishing itself from five geese flying in form.
O the crippled government of love, love, love.
Numb now, why she's just a young thing,
a fillip of the ghostly habit of on and on.

She can barely ride a bike but tomorrow she'll have reason
to remark, The peppercorns have bled the cheese brown.
And across the table, another will note,
The five-fluid-ounce flask has gone missing.

TRAVEL IS EASY BY TRAIN

Don't you love a narrow corridor? Ham asked. Only one way
to get lost, or to find. It was the year of the rat,
shunned overachiever, and late in a day that was long.
The girl in the icy-blue coat gave them her eyes,
only to take them right back.

We're all like her, Louise said, twice ourselves
in a window's reflection, alone on the train.
They watched both sides of a coin as it slipped past
the point of divide. Outside they could see
February's first flowering—a fictional rose, goatsbeard up early.

They listened to inaudible inches mince toward,
unfeasible finches flap toward. It was time for lunch.
They are best, Ham explained, as he plucked figs from a basket,
taken in bites, like bits of tissue gnawed from a vole bone
or consumed like the lone shark

released from the jail bars of a grill bed—swallowed not whole
but maintaining at all costs each bite its bitness
for the textured toboggan ride south.
His napkined neck nodded his head with its pillbox
engraveled with thought.

. . .

So much to ignore, he said, to find flower instead in the fork,
which needs be held in the hand and never let fall
out of flavor. Yes, like that. Of course—he turned
to the other—taste always finds us.
The new, Louise said, blasphemes. You know it does.

A PORTRAIT OF LOVE

Part tea party, part fog in the firs
crowding the shore. The thorn pig advanced,
pork in the pines.

On the porch, Isabella practiced piano for one hand,
her other hand wrapped in a boa, a fluffy flight-
feathered mitt.

Tea and the pitfalls of town, then the conversation
collapsed into an arresting presence.
A backward glance. The dove of her life

fast evaporating into impossibility.
You're funny, aren't you. I always said you were funny.
The dogwood blossoms rose up to meet

the crack under the wall sconce.
From the hallway, a dangerous draft. The unfinished
business of seduction. A flat face in a mirror

framed by prettiness, flame-pink piece of paradise
pleasing the eye but never addressing the why
this why that. In isolation, of course,

. . .

there was purification. The child played
well in spite of a directional malady, loud for soft;
hard for adagietto. The thorn pig advanced, rooting

in a nexus of needles, its pinched face mirrored
in a latent puddle. What does Narcissus see
in that little disk?

THE RAVEN FEEDS REYNARD

Seeded yeast in her beak and bending
down mouth to his mouth. Kisses
mismeant, reversal just lurking. Abrupt and walks off.
An abyss sunders them.
She with a love of the beautiful bordering

on excessive frivolity. He with his science and thievish
propensities. An unnatural bonhomie. He kissed her
wing and folded it
over faux fingers fretted feathers and false
all false and falling.

Mouth to her ticking. Time stopped
in a tea shop. My, doesn't this taste? The repertoire ending
in a dance dress, black and sleek
(Wouldn't Lydia like to see her now, all sisterenvy).
In the morning, left to her lovedream, her rapt regard retrained

onto the window. Is someone rapping? No, the wet wind
rain-veined and soaking the roses. Tomorrow tariffed but still
the labyrinth door swings two ways,
every peril paired with its opposite
until.

WHAT IS A MOUTH?

Steam burst from the opening and hot words,
that sleeve of tea poured through a spout
(a drop plunked on the plate like a huffy ember).

A green fluorescence set in a shallow, some leach
from a reeky hell. She was too earnest, too bird-chirp,
too leaf as lime turned it blue. A terrifying rot

but the teeth of eight Dobermans in downward descent
was what she feared more. Say it ain't so, she said.
Ham said, Sit on the right

to see the river lapse into least resistance. Watch the night
trick the vertical lamp of a gray glass window
back into darkness. This is where I leave it to others,

Louise said, to make sense of that musical motion
at the margin of sight, the razor wire
and other ruthless markers, the axe

wrapped in tree roots. She returned to the city
after hearing obscenities said in the house by the high school
in the dawn of a reasonable doubt.

NIGHT FALLING FAST

Was he gone for good? Or only an hour? Louise could never tell.
His hat was an after-
image fixed to the list of her eye. Was he tall and narrow,
did he wear white socks with black shoes, a fashion forgot-
ten so long ago but recently reborn as retro? Was he missing
to her? Had her heart's heart ever truly been his?

Or did she belong to whomever was wearing her arm
on his neck; her lip's sweetish lavender kiss
still hung in the air-
less room. Night falling fast in a shadowed locale
where a thin line could mean either fact or forensics:
the track of a fracture or the time it might take to wrap up a body.

The China dog tugged at its leash while in the radium light,
center and slightly, a zebra stood standing still.
The day had been ethereal until . . .
And where was the other when she needed a friend
to whom she could lend an ear
in return for a bed that was wider than one?

. . .

Her eyes remained anchored
on some furry distance; a furrow erased from her brow.
Let yourself go, she said to herself, and she did
know how after all. The night continued the day.
A murder of crows went by. What would she have?
The last beloved restored

to canvas and hanging, a knife through his heart?
Or a new who excelled where others had fizzled to Fail,
floundering fish on a shoal. Let go the leash
of the bad dogs that are dragging you this way and that.
And indeed, the hand could unclasp (Look at that!).
The leash fell at her feet.

Across the room, five fish in a tank made six meager moves,
the last through the castle that kept them
denizens of a splendid
language they spoke sotto voce.

DARK SMUDGED THE
PATH UNTRAMMELED

The room was warm, sugar sweet, and wormwood bitter
with radiators trimmed in half-shell

heading cast columns looking unlikely
to support their visual weight. How easy,

said Louise, it is to be crushed.
They were twelve at the table, six on each side.

A tableau untainted by paint, an even jury
sitting in judgment.

She could hear music—was it the spheres?
Planets passing Adam's sarcophagus, bowing down in what?

Honor? Or relief that they were diviner matter,
a test doctrine as yet unbested. It was time

for dessert: pie, a structural lemon, cloud-coated
with a Corinthian cap formed of feathers

standing at wistful attention. There was no see deeper
than this—the very sight kept them submerged

. . .

and they swam like skylarks straining to locate
a star without the help of the sky.

To the one on her right, Louise said no, she would not sit
for his dog—a taffy-toned poodle with a puppy cut

that answered to the name of Roy.
She would be away that week, grazing a coast

before entering a sea, taking a sloop, sipping her tea.
Adrift. Besides, she said, she could never be anyone's

My Dear Girl. She would never respond
to a call from a telephone held to a distant, indifferent ear.

She was, in a word, not-his-type, and then she turned
to her left, a sinister shift, and in her best whisper

she asked to be taken home. Bye, they said. Bye-bye.
The late hours were arriving, car after car.

A HURRICRANIUM, HE SAID

Rain on the outside, horror on the in.
That wind could cause such
alases and sighs but there was no resignation, no.

Knee deep in distant duck honk. What a waterway.
What a what would I have done in that one's space?
It was an anniversary of sorts of the sound

of song sung once in a bitty chapel far overseas.
O 'twas England. This isn't Eden, she'd said. Eat or be eaten.
And he put it to music. O 'twas

BEAUTIFUL. O 'twas a song for all reasons. 'Twasn't it?
Now he was silent. Has the cat got your whether? he asked.
And indeed, she had seen a cat, bedraggled as a rock badger

fresh from the stream between two fallowed fields.
Now there you go again, he said,
relying on Nature. A lie, she said. *Menteur.*

. . .

He turned his head and half hid behind his hand
because who could look—the tall trees swished like Death
batting its lush purple lashes.

The very sound was wearying. They were the inside
wishing to be out. Would the rain fade, finally, and allow them
to state alas at last? And sing again.

CAPTIVITY

Those birds will eat anything—
the carcass subsumed in death, the heart convulsing
in laughter. So this is how it ends, a dart in the eye
of Ifdom. The duck grows
up to be a pillow, the table takes the tree
out for a talk—We must stop meeting like this.
And that arrowed water on which the women row?
Oh, dangerous, yes. At any moment an arm can reach up
and show the wrong side of the dice. And then
where will they be? Children again
before boredom and invention awaiting some birthdom.
A tiny thumb stuck in the port.
That kind of desolation can double as solace, Louise said.
Yes, the skeleton dreaming its body back to a particular
limit—a lovely skin, a mind that knows nothing
of boundaries, the erotic singsong of motion.
The happy little cage.

THEY CHIRP, THEY WHISTLE, AND WORDS

In this volume, green as even odds, we see so little of victory,
  Ham said.

The story of mighty fallen. How are they now? Ward of no man.
  Ward of any.

Under the washer, the smell of slippery water puddling the
vase hour, flat as the world before it was.

In the afterwards, fireworks, the dusty air floating small store-pink.

The hand holding the icy pop can.

A carpet of packed dirt and bare feet beiged by dust.

One had no name but he sang. All day all night. They kissed, of
  course.

The play will not go forward, he said, and it didn't despite their
  tears.

Despite decline. The day proceeded dumb.

Louise was to have played spring and advanced
across the stage in a bit of a slink. But it were not to be so.
. . .

After that she felt her frail fortune reversing; she grew more and
    more a picture.

Finally the day turned dark brown, bountifully beautiful.

The rabbits were happy.

A clutch of cackling hens with their fat young cheeks crossed
the road in front of them.

Why are they crossing? Ham asked.

Why indeed. Charles Gordon called her an owl and she didn't
    object.

Waking at night, skirting the damp floor of the forest.

Leaving a feather caught in the foxglove.

Foraging for a view through the prism of nature.

INCONSEQUENT MOMENT

Time standing quite, quite still, reflecting back
possibility like tall mirrors sometimes send back laid tables,
napkins cresting on the swell of violas.

Orchids for the ladies, gardenias for the gents.
A silence drew across them, a solid propagation of empty O's.
The scene studied its own picture postcardism, then an adroit
    change

of conversation to a recent imbroglio
of kittens found in a kitchen box.
Mountain to molehill.

Charles Gordon began to sing a song
she'd heard before, "For Those in Danger on the Sea."
Time stood still.

Studied vagueness for the ladies, long looks for the gents.
The latter, cunning and subtle, conducive to misery.
Summer-dusty motorcars in a garden

of wallflowers walled in by yews. Louise was distracted
for a moment
by the extravagant delving of a duck beneath her skirt.
. . .

O Nature! A glance held a jay in its hand. Vines intertwined
between minutes. Misery or a bad shock can make a mind go
     blank,
she thought. Well, there you are. There they were.

She recalled the day
she had followed a man with fair red hair
the better part of two miles back to what might have been

but for the fact of it being made of air. A trifle risky, the
reverie. Onyx dreams of ships in fog hooting their horns.
The duck was being nice and neighborly now, putting its back up

to be petted. And Louise and Charles, having little
in common except for an undaunted love
of lightning

and live wire, looked at each other and saw
not similarity but distinction
and difference.

ETCHED, TETCHED, TOUCHED

It was perhaps Hollandish. A tinted print
of a functional waterway tearing a town apart.
Aproned ladies and laddies in breeches.

A dog baited by a strip of bacon. Louise didn't care
for such scenes. Static antics, she said. Sterile takes
on quotidian twilight.

Give me rapture and bliss, she told Ham.
Hieronymus Bosch and Mister S. Dalí
(her sister Lydia claimed to have seen the latter

her second summer in Montmartre).
The epiphany of Yves Tanguy walking a panther
seaside in Cannes.

Such sights call up the shades, Louise said.
Only they know how to last.
Meaning, forever.

All else shifts the way the print has now tilted
with no one near.
Ham crossed the carpet to right it.

. . .

Of course, Louise too could be a pretty picture: a woman
riveted to earth in raiments
right for the season—hilarity on her face,

the boat balanced behind her. From another angle
a perilous island
of plenty volcanic—tigers hidden in treetops,

leopards masking the faces
of mountains—an irresistible silence on the edge
of a ruin, warm at the wrist.

IN THE QUIETER AFTERMATH

Of course it's an explosion, the number seven
flying off to the north, cat's whiskers to the east,
a checkerboard dead center staying put to confound her.
Today is a tantrum—*detto diluvio*.
One cat looks one way; the other, the other.
She is an imaginary city
consistent with a style of progressive architecture.
She was never destined for a pure reality.
Come rivolta non importa.
Yes, she's electric and yes,
she's a monster
at times.
Now *verticale*
now *orizzontale*
now *equilibrio*
now *silenzio.*

How simple she looks
riding a bike. How simple she sees
what she sees. She could be a camera,
each eye a little leaf shutter, angles falling over themselves
until blankness. When stripped of light she is decidedly less.
Diminished to fewer than few, to cat whiskers cut on a bias—
O now see the mice play their game of croquet
on the unswept dining room carpet.

ON TO THE ONSLAUGHT: A LITTLE MILLENNIAL DIRGE

1.

And here, where the pin pricked the silken red rib
Louise's pen was at the port of turning to—yes,
mum; no, mum. Her mother had said, Don't talk
to me like that, young lady. Lady Grey grew tired
of looking out her little window. The port
of turning back to the world with a sense of revulsion.
Progress, Louise said, is a slow evolution. One pads along,
plots a great gong, then waits for the next devolution.
Are we too many? she asked. There was a lamp
at the end of the funnel. Let's stand—she gestured to the dis-
    tance—
at the counter. There she divided the days:
one for you, one for me, and one for the girl with the ruby
    tattoo.

2.

The lights in the trees made a cat's cradle
of the lines they had used to define them. Wand world,
word elision. Happy was the stiff
birch, snappy the branches in the tree wind. Rewind, she said,
and you'll see the gray slate of autumn, astray
from an off-center center. O kiss the night that it comes up
so often and blanks out what surrounds the lampposts,

leaving only the camp mid-song. The cowboy and cowgirl
drinking their evening Madeira.

The wire wrapping them keeps wrapping, choking the poster-girl
blond until she coughs up a quick succession of three over four
divided by dawn. It breaks, said Louise, because it won't bend.

RITUAL GESTURES

Night closes over. Voltaire knocks
at his daughter's window but finds instead Louise
and Lydia locked in each other's arms—
brilliant in tears, in tumult, unaccustomed to tragedy.
Audible only to V in his ghostcoat, they vow
all is forgiven in the sisterspat. L takes a flower
from her hair and gives it to L.
The other does likewise and thus
the sorority is mended. Self is safe. Pain lulled at least.
Pale, one taps her forehead once; the other twice, not a riposte
but an idiolect developed in the early days
when they were but twee girls dressed alike and spoke little and
    late.
Each window locked three times, one for comfort
and twice for fear.

SO THIS

So this is reality—a ghostscape in the afterstorm,
the lake lit white with lightning. A mouth open
in a yawn. Children, children, sit here. Near.
Louise and Lydia both wearing the same blue dress
trimmed with white ribbon, a bow on each shoulder.
The long-suffering dog lets Louise (as you can see,
the taller by sight) sit on his back. She is his most beloved
and he is hers. A shoe, a sock, an arm
on the back of a sofa. So, reality. Wind and water.
Louise with her hair pulled back, Lydia with a veil.
Fruit and fish, a flat dish rimmed with seashells.
Maple leaf and myth. Ophelia.
The bed, the bottle, the dog, the cat, the elephant
blanketed red in a circular scene. And now—
the foot is lifted, the trunk is lofted, and sound
fills the air and now the pear tree, the Palais de Pape,
the pool table. Lydia with a hat, Louise with a bat
and ball. A game of badminton, a day of croquet,
a crown of sonnets, or terrible thorns. Fruit
rimmed with seashells, a fish with two feet.
The long-suffering sofa. A circular scene: the bull enters
the ring. The myth of man's disobedience.
Louise on a lake, shoes light wet with white rain.
Lydia like Ophelia, her face in a flower. A frond.
A frond. A tangle of twos. A terrible knot.

THE STILL KNIFE STILL SUSPENDED

From where she sat she could see
a sundial, but she couldn't read it. Time was
a brushfire burning somewheres, haze
on a distant waterplay. Small but mighty birds
raked a rattle across a slate. Behind the hedge, she sensed
a shadow pacing. Panther? Or Pavlovian?
Evening would find her, ivy wrapping her
delicate ankles. A church bell rang once.
The invisible vicar lit a candle and cursed
the beggars who loitered noisily outside.
A tide moved. In the sky, strange Sirius.
Siren girls sang somewhere. A boat rocked. She could see
nothing, really. No clairvoyant forecasts.
Did dark descend? No. Dark seeps womb to wind
through tiny vessels underneath the epiderm
and tangle with nighttime. Hello? It was the Pavlovian
and here he was. Barking at the fruitless peach tree
defuncted how long now? Surely years.
She thought of a clockface in the form of decision,
peach-tinted mother-of-pearl. She had seen it in a shop
at the corner of Eighth and E. Sunlit smoke flitted
behind the bell tower. The boat backtreaded the current.
A mouse caught by a kitten was just then released and ran by.

LYDIA'S SUITE: ONE WITHOUT HAS TWO OR THREE WITHIN

1. O DEJECTION

Eight brown leaves lay in the tight right angle
at the millennial end
of a bright blue pool. Nine high windows.

A star store darkened for the duration.
In a bad-berry year, she said, the bears lumber
out from the forest, drape themselves in the barked sticks

of stark trees in the light of a universe
formed by scratched arms and harmed curios
in the cabinet, a watch aglow on a nightstand.

It had been a bad-berry year,
her slatted ribs were taut in their empty tent.
Lydia said she loved the little mirrors,

the miniature furniture of nothing but face and no notice
of an emaciated frame. How tired she was now, how
deeply drugged on daily sorrows.

2. TO RETAIN THE ARRANGEMENT

Sorrow lodged in the corner of a mouth, saliva-wet.
The flimsy partition between said and thought.
The city on the horizon disappears.
The shuffle outside the door ceases.
In every landscape there are enigmatic elements
if one cares to call them that, Louise said.
A glove with a buckle, a belt with a crocodile head,
its tail turned toward the light.
A gardenia bouquet giving off the effluvia of decay.
Inkish matter rubbing dark the wrist.
Myself at the Age of When, she said.
That was the name of the film she fancied this was,
or would be if left in the wrong hands.
It was seven o'clock and dusk dusted the anteroom alibi gray.
Lydia said she was going out and not to wait late
because she might not return.
Her hand became a scar on the doorknob,
turning forever and ever in the center of the stalled summer
    month.

3. SHE WENT OUT INTO THE CLEAR COAST

And saw, in a shop window, glasses piled in a pyramid.
An unstable beam of light at the corner captured a column
of steam escaping a pipe. She blinked.
The requisite reexamination—life flashing like a broken brick
caught in the crossfire of two trains at right angles
each coming and coming to the same point,
retracting the threat from the threat of death.
In through the glass-topped door, she switched on the lights
in successive rooms.
There was menace in the soft carpets, clocks
and screens, china dogs held by painted chains,
all handled by the low-key light of a lamp.
The aspidistra looked lovely with its handsome leaves
and 4-merous flowers. Lydia said
to herself, This
is the moment of decision. The banal fixed
like a hand on a banister, a weak ineffectual figure positioned
and lit, her mouth open in a tiny scream too small to alert
the cardboard characters lolling beneath a streetlight outside.
She had been here before but fear had always fractured her
from the moment of release. Now she was laying out her best
black dress, now the little that went underneath.
Shoes, stockings. The arm of the chair
could barely contain this trousseau. To leave and leaving
to be left undecided.

4. EXQUISITE CORPSE

The annihilation of the well-behaved
one. White placed
and pulled over the face. Louise saddened past sobbing
knife turn in the neck of grief.
I cannot, she said, but could not
speak more. And Ham knowing too much
how it happened. Silent now. Knife turn in the neck
of on-going. And the other, at the height of hysteria.
A pill given and swallowed with water.
A mention of murder
but knowledge was missing.
Nothing was missing, a birthstone borrowed
was there on the nightstand. But no note.
No terrible note noting particular sorrows.
No cannot go on. Mystery and a miss
who was now carried out,
placed in a carriage and called someone was calling
but no one knew where
they would take her. She was taken.
She was and was now
no more of her. She was as exquisite as ever
the diggers did see. And they had seen much.
And they had seen many.

5. NIGHT AND NAIL

That small feathered fiend, the needle that goes through you.
The beak threading through pity, the thread threading pity
to the porcelain cheek, a line where it lay on the bedsheet
all morning. Love forlorn and belled, a cat clattering
as far as China, as near as here. The dim reaches
of a watchdog's yawn, enter there if you dare.
A foot trips at the incisor's edge. O going
down a tunnel. Any dream merchant worth her salt will tell you
to follow each bead until you come to
and there a spooned portion:

a potion not really bitter but bland,
baited with a bit of *sel gris*. She wasn't having any,
if you know what I mean. No mused rhyme could buy back
what had been bought or sold, bagged or borrowed. Sentiment
no bigger than a bauble. Disillusionment in the back of a cab.

Music from somewhere, an all-night Bird song—sweet, sweet,
sweet. The murmurous flaunt of heavenly high notes.
    Perplexing breezes
bleeding through the casement. The fled anthem fading. O
    Baby O!
Coming back to the thread now wrapping the wrist.
Passion a snare to hope.

From a single nail on the blank wall hung many of several
images—Bird, notes, Heaven, tender
tomorrow's green-leached leaves, specter-thin. The Moon em-
    balmed
in Egypt, gloating above the sphinx. The thread was a path-
as-well, down which one could travel, hand to a handle,
descending into ceaseful Death. But one would take nothing
    with.
No book in which the dotted sand glowed relentlessly
behind the inky type. No sorry folded note that said.
No consoling tinnitus against the empty sound. No perfume
of great magnitude and marble. Does she wake? Or will we
    weep?

6. ENCHAINED

Let Death be concrete, a dream
of dual Dalmatians standing in the scattered mass,
of pure puce shirts and shattered curses.
The smell of lilac. The sight holding
even what went out to sea at the end of the day,
serial monosyllables the ear hears. O little closure
we have looked for you
everywhere and yet
you give back so small a bit when we do find you—
a whittled kiss, one cheek, two,
the cycle soothes like sleep. Oh, very,
very like. Sheepish she looked through
her fringe for hadn't she just woke
from a scene so macabre. That they might not know
she was now new would not occur to her she so was one
with them. Much have I travell'd, she thought to say,
but what good. She was now and new.
A zero, slashed through but not canceled. This
is what it is to wake
to a bell that says what it wants.
The hearing of it meant so much. In Death
the eyes might see, yes, but would the ear hear?
Doubt it. The Dalmatians barkless as a tree.
First looked at. First looked into.

RAPTURED

A full moon at the moment of perigee, after the sun
had been south and shining
down on a frowning Tropic of Capricorn.
Where they were, the days were shortest, nights longest;
a flooded coast was possible, a fallen star
had been seen. Where have you been?
the other asked. It was a difficult question.
Louise stood tall and, instead of an answer, said,
Sheep feed, and pointed to the unruly grass.
Quack, went a duck. The farmhouse was full,
every room fitted out in finest array.
Sweet Isabellita had finished her food and now played
not with a doll but a small pink flamingo.
Charles Gordon, as usual, was playing the fool.
Someone was sure to announce soon
that, the day being more or less done, it was time
to concede, to accept,
that little loss that the clockface maintained,
the gone that O echoed over and over as it walked
on the edge of apology. Ham summoned her
into the house. She was in a most cooperative mood,
a late state of appreciation. She carried, in one hand, a copy
of *Mrs. Dalloway;* in the other, a fistful of blooms
she'd retrieved from the foggy shore of the twining river.
It was cool. There was moss on the rock wall
the same shrill color of the hooded coat she wore.

That too was in the family of rapture, every twinning bit
of what made up the murmur of the scaffolding folding itself
into itself. *And with poor skill let pass into the breeze
the dull shell's echo.* With a honk and a hoot,
a car pulled into the drive and Lydia stepped out.
They all came running to greet her, to tell what must be told,
and tell it well, omitting what didn't matter
to one who had missed the day. Where had she been?
they all asked, when she had settled into a chair
in front of a billowing fire. Where, indeed!
I dreamed, she said, my death;
an ambulance and a man named Dan
took me to a morgue and you were all there, at least you
    three—
she gestured to Ham, Louise, and Charles G.
Her audience sat in stunned silence as she continued
her uncommon tale of descent and ascension
into a patient brilliance. Light, said Louise.
Not quite, said Lydia. For it was beyond saying, this sense
of sudden change. All the same, she attempted
to describe the effect: Like basking, she said, in the end
that is no end at all but is more like an endless beginning.
Some looked vexed but Louise understood.
For wasn't that her story as well? Wasn't that the story
she'd been retelling into some dear's ear
for what seemed now forever? Wasn't that the small car

that changed color as it passed on its way to the zoo?
Wasn't that the kiss on the eyelids by sleep as it opened
the door to excess? There one was quite likely to meet
an okapi on a long leash, the zookeeper out for a walk.
The lovey-dovey muddlement of an arbitrary set
of bizarre incidents. Hunting in a fluted skirt for another farewell,
Louise thought. From a vase, the roses stared
like oxen. The air was gin-clear. On closer inspection,
the flowers were artificial, cut from sardine tins.
The two terriers, Autumn and Autumn, were wrapped
in a haze of giving. Each a cake
of soap holding the hand that had shaped it.

HAM PAINTS A PICTURE TO ILLUSTRATE
AN EARLY LESSON: O TRAUMA!

He remembered the dog bite. The door
opened and, under the host, the hostess,
their faces unfrowned, both dressed in brown,

the dog. And happy to be seen
by a boy such as that. So small.
And so sudden. A bite

as a blur, a blow, pierce puncture red-wrought and tears.
Were there? The highest ideal of unwelcome
and now denuded of calm, air ripe with arrested attention,

yes, tears, one for each toothmark arrayed in two rows.
Formally speaking, one step to the side
of the rhetoric of sympathy. The terrier tense and shut off

now from the party had had his six shots, had he not?
He had, but what
of the boy—wee fellow—memory now marred by what can't be
    extracted

as there is no such instrument, no so sharp a knife,
no drug nor attar into which it will meld
a marbleized batter, so pretty the cake.

. . .

The party keeps on, its snug details melted
to a telling without any tale,
only pain out of nowhere to no one he now knew

but one he had been. So it was, so it is.
Heedless hallucination
(re)seeded in a narrative setting.

Dog. Bite. The sublime scenery
of host and hostess, the mother
a diminutive presence, protectress unforgiven

for the lapse. What is done to one.
Something. Terrible. That pain must be
endured alone. The residue

of a certainty residing as the remote so-called
(recalled) picture. Image, can one say? One can say anything
one likes but here the less said the better, he said

to himself, no longer speaking
of what can be bloodied but something less liquish,
love—Oh, what a word!

INTERRUPTED BRIEFLY BY A BORROWED
PHRASE, THE SCENE PROCEEDS

Around a tabletop scattered with ruins, the abbey
of an ate cake, one wall still standing
but angling in a bit, crumb *comme* rock dotting the sandscape

of a handmade plate.
What a party it were and one played the birthday boy.
O October! Seeds of spent summer

plashing the weather vane. Late the sky
shifting to lavender, a touch of rain
in the pained face of she who had been betrayed

by the celebrant. Now holding a flute
of champagne and tipping a rim
toward Louise, a tiny tap-tap, *chin-chin,*

a hollow toast, the host rising
to say a few words, a wish for wonderment
All Year Long. What a thing!

But oh! how unlike marble was that face.
How beautiful, if Sorrow had not made
Sorrow more beautiful than Beauty's Self.

. . .

Now she rose and touching a fingertip to her cold lips
gestured for silence to fall
under the canopy that covered them,

that affirmed their right to be each in their own
flamboyant drama. None could be released now—
not by syncope nor the light tap that disturbs

the hypnotic's shallow nap.
In other words, the boat could not be capsized
as long as someone listened.

THEY WERE THAT AND THEN

They moved
into the interior. Torn from the frou-frou
of jaboted mirrors and shuffled chairs,
a dominating card table on spindly dog legs, they moved
into the electric connections
that traipsed the chasm between synaptic clefts.
They moved into the mind
your p's and q's, into the light
that no light brights,
into the brain's back of the hand on which is run the movie
of the moment—now and now, now and then,
now and when. They moved blindly backwards
and away from the text that failed to find their eyes.
They would eventually be weighed
in the blue comparison pool, unadjectived,
unmetaphored, unmineraled of earth mire.
They would be unmanned, unwomanned, unothered.
Diamond beams rising from steamy beakers, they would rest
on a metal cart rolling down a clean corridor
blank in a khaki noon. Empty.
Nothing. Good for nothink. And feeling
they had forever been so.
So unlike the logic of the lamp.